Wolfgang Giovanni Constance

Italian in 10 days

Language course with a new
method

AF189730

Publishing house:
Books on Demand
Norderstedt, Germany
ISBN 9783748128601
© 2018 Wolfgang Giovanni Constance
Cover: San Lorenzo, Florence
Photo: Wolfgang Giovanni Constance

Table of contents

First day

The pronunciation

How to learn the pronunciation: If you translate an English text into Italian at Google, you can then **listen to the Italian text**.

A stressed sound is in bold.

<u>Vowels</u>

	explanation	example
a	long like a in park	
e	open like e in bet	b**e**ne / well
	closed like e in the word they (without the final i glide)	
		s**e**ra / evening
i	like ee in street	**i**sola / island
	before and between vowels like y in young	
		fi**o**re / flower
o	open like o in pot	per**ò** / but
	closed like o in post	s**o**le / sun
u	like oo in good	**u**no / one

<u>Consonants</u>

	explanation	example
c	before e and i like ch in much	
		c**e**na / dinner
	otherwise like c in casino	
		c**a**sa / house

ch	like c in casino	**a**nche / also
g	before e and i like **g** in **g**entleman	
		giorno / day
	otherwise like g in gold g**u**sto/taste	
gh	like g in gold	spagh**e**tti
gn	like **ny** in can**y**on	sig**n**ora / Mrs.
gli	like **lli** in mi**lli**on	**fi**glio / son
h	h is always silent	ho / I have
r	rolled r	**R**oma / Rome
qu	c like c in car + u like oo in good	
		qu**i** / here
s	between vowels like **s** in is	
		chiesa /church
	otherwise like s in see	
		s**o**le / sun
sc	before e and i like sh in shop	
		us**c**ita / exit
	otherwise like **sk** in **sk**i	
		s**c**onto/discount
z	at the beginning of words	
	like ds in pads	**z**ucchero / sugar
	otherwise like ts in cats	
		gra**z**ie / thanks

Italian alphabet

A (a), B (bee), C (cee), D (dee), E (e), F(efe)G (gee), H (aka),I (ee), K (kapa), L (elle), M (eme), N (ene), O (o), P (pee) Q (coo), R (ere), S (ese), T (tee), U (oo), V (voo), W (voo dopeea), X (eex), Y (eepsee lon), Z (dseta)

Accents

Usually the penultimate syllabe is stresssed.

Last syllabe: stressed with two accents:

1. L'accento grave: open pronunciation:caffè
2. L'accento acuto: closed pronunciation: perché / why?

In addition, the accent is used to distinguish between identical words, for example: sì / yes and si / one, themselves

Abbreviations

derivation of the grammatical rules	D
example	EX
optional part	**OP**
past participle	PP
plural	Pl
singular	Sg
rule	R
masculine	m
feminine	f

I controllo doganale / The customs check

Luogo: L'aeroporto Leonardo da Vinci a Roma.
Place: The airport Leonardo da Vinci in Rome
A tourist T, customs officer

O Buon pomeriggio. Good afternoon. Il suo passaporto per favore. Your passport please …

Il passaporto è scaduto. The passport has expired.

T Ecco la carta d'identità. This is my identity card. Ho viaggiato molto tempo per l'Inghilterra. I have been travelling for a long time in England. C'è qualcosa di nuovo in Italia? Is there anything new in Italy?

O Non so. I don't know. Ha <u>qualcosa</u> da dichiarare? Do you have <u>anything</u> to declare?

T Non ho niente da dichiarare. I don't have anything to declare.

O Apra questa valigia! Open this case! Ora so qualcosa di nuovo per Lei. Now I know something new for you. Deve pagare il dazio per questo! You have to pay duty on this.

T Ma questo è un regalo. But this is a gift.

O Per chi? For whom?

T Per Lei. For you.

O Grazie mille. Thank you very much.

The underlined words have the same meaning.

Please read the grammar section first in the following chapters and then the short story.

Please learn the underlined words from <u>accident</u> to <u>car.</u>

Second day

Dov'è la stazione / Where is the station?

Place: Rome
A tourist T, passer-by P

T   Mi scusi, Signora. Excuse me madam.
Potrebbe darmi delle informazioni?
Could you give me some information?
Dov'è la stazione? Where is the station?
P   Nel centro città. In the city centre.
T   Ci posso andare a piedi? Can I go there
on foot?
P   Non è possibile perché è troppo lontano.
It is not possible because it is too far. La
stazione dista 10 km da qui. The station
is ten kilometres from here.
T   Come si arriva alla stazione? How do
you get to the station?
P   Preferisce l'autobus o la metro? Do you
prefer bus or underground? Tutti e due
vanno alla stazione. Both of them go to
the station.
T   È uguale. I do not mind. Dove è la fermata dell'autobus o la stazione della
metro? Where is the bus stop or the underground station?
P   Ecco la fermata dell'autobus. There is
the bus stop.
T   Quale autobus va alla stazione? Which

bus goes to the station?

P   Penso che sia il numero undici. I think it is the bus number eleven.

T   Quante fermate ci sono fino alla stazione? How many stops are there until the station?

P   Mi dispiace, non lo so. Sorry, I don't know.

T   Non importa. It does not matter. Grazie. Thank you.

The Definite article

EX The boy and the girlfriend go to the spectacle and the zoo.
   Il ragazzo e **l'**amica (1) visitano **lo spett**acolo e **lo z**oo (2).

D   There are two definite articles:
   Sg (m): **il**, (f) **la**
   Before a **vowel** il and la > **l'**. (1)
   Before **s** + **consonant** and **z**: il > **lo**.(2)

Pl   **I** ragazzi e **le** amiche (3) visitano **gli** spettacoli e **gli** zoo. (4)
   The boys and the girlfriends go to the spectacles and the zoos.

D   Pl (m): **i** (f): **le**
   In the plural: **l'** (f) > **le** (3), **l'** (m) > **gli** (before i: gl') and **lo > gli** (4).

R   **The article form is determined by the initial sound of the noun**.
   Gender and number of the article are determined by the noun.

10

OP The Definite Article and its uses

1. Names of countries and regions
    (l'Italia / Italy, La Toscana / Tuscany).
2. Before the adjective possessive (La mia
    casa / my house).
3. For details of ownership with avere /
    have (avere l'auto / have a car).
4. For information of diseases with avere
    (ho il mal di testa / I have a headache)
5. For details of occupations with fare /
    make (faccio il dottore / I am a doctor).
6. When specifying a language (studiare il
    francese / learn French).

OP The Definite Article and family
members

EX My brother, my sisters and my dear
mother.
Mio fratello, **le** mie sorelle e **la** mia
cara mamma.
D   Without definite article: family
member (Sg).
With definite article:
family members (Pl)
family member + **adjective**.

OP The Definite Article after tutto

EX All the three drink all the days a little
wine.

Tutti **e** tre b<u>e</u>vono tutti **i** giorni un po'
di vino.

D   Between tutto and a number: **e**
**Between tutto and a noun: the
definite article**
Between un po' and a noun: **di**

The Partitive Article

EX   Do you want beer / desidera (di+la>)
della birra?(1)
I don't want beer / non desidero **di**
birra. (2)
I want a glass of wine / desidero un
bicchiere **di** vino. (3)

D   Indeterminate quantity: **di + the definite article** (so-called **partitive
article**). (1)
After a verb in the negative (2) and
after a determinate quantity (3):
only **di**.

The definite article and prepositions

	il	lo	la	l'	i	gli	le
di / of	**del**	dello	della	dell'	dei	degli	delle
da / by	dal	dallo	dalla	dall'	dai	dagli	dalle
a / to,at	**al**	allo	alla	all'	ai	agli	alle
in / in	nel	nello	nella	nell'	nei	negli	nelle
su on	sul	sullo	sulla	sull'	sui	sugli	sulle

The Indefinite Article

EX A boy and a girlfriend go to a spectacle
     and a zoo.
     Un ragazzo e **un'**amica (1) visitano
     uno spettacolo e **uno** **z**oo (2).

D   Sg (m): **un** (f): **una**
     Before a **vowel**: una > **un'**. (1)
     Before **s+consonant** and **z**: un > **uno**
     (2)

Pl Boys and girlfriends go to spectacles
     and zoos.
     Dei ragazzi e **delle** amiche visitano
     degli spettacoli e **degli** **z**oo.(3)

D   Pl (m): **dei** (f): **delle**
     dei before **s+consonant** and **z** > **degli**.
     (3)

R   **The article form is determined by**
     the initial sound of the main word.

R   The **plural form** is **not translated**.

Mr C… and Mrs H…

Place: Rome

C   How are you? Come sta?
H   Fine thanks and you? Gr**a**zie, va bene e
     Lei?
C   My name is Cock. Mi chiamo Cock.
     What is your name? Come si chi**a**ma?
H   My nam is Hen. Mi chi**a**mo Hen.
C   Pleased to meet you. Piac**e**re. Where are

you from? Lei di dov'è?

H I am from Britain. Sono d'Ingilterra.

C My ancestors are from Britain too. I miei
antenati sono venuti d'Inghilterra anche.

H I am sorry, I have to go now. Mi dispiace, adesso devo partire. It was nice meeting you Mr Cock. È stato un piacere conoscervi, Signor Cock.

C Goodbye, Mrs Hen, have a good return
Arrivederci, Signora Hen, buon ritorno.

Conjugation

avere / to have and essere / to be

Present	ho (1)	sono(2)	I am
1 I have	hai	sei	you are
2 I am	ha	è	he is
	abbiamo	siamo	we are
	avete	siete	you are
	hanno	sono	they are
PP	avuto / had	stato / been	

OP

Imperfect	avev-o (1)	er-o (2)
1 I had	-i	-i
2 I was	-a	-a
	-amo	erav-amo
	-ate	erav-ate
	-ano	er-ano

14

Future	av-**rò** (1)	sa-**rò** (2)
1 I will have	**-rai**	**-rai**
2 I will be	**- rà**	**-rà**
	- remo	**-remo**
	-rete	**-rete**
	-ranno	**-ranno**

Conditional	av-**rei** (1)	sa-**rei** (2)
1 I would	**-resti**	**-resti**
have	**-rebbe**	**-rebbe**
2 I would	**-remmo**	**-remmo**
be	**-reste**	**-reste**
	-rebbero	**-rebbero**

OP Similar words

action	azione f
annual	annuale
cause	causa f
collection	collezione f
color	colore m
commercial	commerciale
cost	costo m
delicious	delizioso
figure	figura f
famous	famoso
generous	generoso
geography	geografia f
history	storia f
list	lista f
medicine	medicina f

The Cardinal Numbers

0	zero		
1	uno	11	**u**ndici
2	due	12	do**d**ici
3	tre	13	tre**d**ici
4	quattro	14	quattordici
5	cinque	15	qu**i**ndici
6	sei	16	se**d**ici
7	sette	17	diciasette
8	otto	18	dici**o**tto
9	nove	19	dicianove
10	dieci	20	venti

From 20 to 100, the basic numbers are always formed according to the same pattern. The decimal number is supplemented by the numbers 1 - 9. The decimal number loses its final vowel when the following number begins with a vowel, for example

20 venti
21 venti-uno > vent**u**no
22 ventid**ue**
28 venti-otto > vent**o**tto
29 ventin**o**ve
30 trenta
40 quar**a**nta
50 cinqu**a**nta
60 sess**a**nta
70 sett**a**nta
80 ott**a**nta
90 nov**a**nta
100 cento

16

200 due cento
1 000 mille
2 000 due mila
10 000 dieci mila
100 000 cento mila
1000000 un milione

OP The Ordinal Numbers and the Fractions

first	il primo, la prima	
second	secondo	**1/2:**
un mezzo		
third	terzo	1/3:
un terzo		
fourth	quarto	1/4:
un quarto		
fifth	quinto	1/5:
un quinto		
sixth	sesto	
seventh	settimo	
eighth	ottavo	
ninth	nono	
tenth	decimo	1/10:
un decimo		

From 11. the ordinal numbers are always formed according to the same pattern: The basic numbers are supplemented by the suffix -esimo, whereby the basic number loses its final vowel, since the ending -esimo begins with a vowel, for example 11. undici--esimo > undicesimo.For the fractions one uses the ordinal numbers.

Exception: ½ un mezzo

OP <u>What time is it?</u>

At the time is added to the colloquial up to 39 minutes, deducted from the 40th minute of the next hour.

What time is it? Che ore sono?

1.00 È l'una 1.10 l'una e dieci 1.15 l'una e un quarto 1.30 l'una e un mezzo 1.39 l'una e trentanove 1.40 sono le due meno venti 1.45 sono le due meno un quarto 2.00 sono le due

OP <u>What's the date today</u>?

Quanti ne abbiamo oggi / What's the date today?

Oggi è il **primo** gennaio. Today is the first January.

Il **tre** Gennaio vado a Roma. The third January I go to Rome.

D First day: ordinal number, the other days cardinal numbers.

OP <u>Irregular Verbs</u>

bere / drink

Present: bevo bevi beve beviamo bevete bevono

PP: bevuto

cadere / fall

cado cadi cade cadiamo cadete cadono

PP: caduto

Please learn the underlined words from <u>carry</u> to <u>cup</u>.

Third day

Lo sciopero / the strike

Luogo: La stazione centrale di Milano
Location: the central station of Milan
A tourist T, employee E

T (davanti allo sportello / in front of the
  ticket office): Quando parte il prossimo
  treno per Roma? When does the next
  train leave for Rome?
E Non lo so. I do not know. <u>Da ieri</u> invece
  dell'orario abbiamo uno sciopero. Instead
  of the time table we have been on strike
  <u>since yesterday</u>.
T Da dove parte il treno? Where does the
  train leave from?
E Dal binario sei. From platform six.
T Devo cambiare treno? Do I have to
  change trains?
E Sì, deve cambiare treno a Firenze. Yes,
  you have to change trains at Florence.
T Riusciro a prendere la coincidenza per
  Roma? Will I catch my connection to
  Rome?
E Certo che no. Certainly not.
T Quanto tempo dura il viaggio? How
  long does the journey last?
E Normalmente tre ore, ma oggi per lo
  sciopero sei ore.

Normally three hours, but today because
of the strike six hours.

T C'è una carrozza cuccette? Is there a
couchette?

E Sì, ma per lo sciopero solo fino a Firenze. Yes, but because of the strike
only until Florence.

T Vorrei prenotare un posto vicino al fi-
nestrino e una cuccetta. I would like to
 reserve a window seat and a couchette.
Per favore un biglietto di seconda classe,
andata e ritorno, il ritorno senza sciopero.
Please give me a second - class return
ticket. The return journey without the
strike.

The noun

Plural and Gender

EX The boy loves the girlfriend all night
long.
Il ragazzo ama la ragazza tutta la notte.

Pl I ragazzi amano le ragazze tutte le
notti.

D In the plural -o becomes -i, -a > -e and
-e > -i.

R Nouns ending in o: gender mostly m
Nouns ending in a: gender mostly f
Nouns ending in e: gender m or f

R   Nouns ending in **-ione**: gender mostly
     f, for ex.
     (la pensione / the pension).
R   Nouns ending in **-ista**: gender m or f,
     for ex.
     il, la turista / the tourist.
R   In Italian, there are **only female and
     male nouns**.

   OP The same Plural and Singular

EX   On the photo you see the tram in the
     city.
     Sulla **foto** si vede il **tram** nella **città**.
PL   Sulle **foto** si vedono i **tram** nelle **città**.
D   The same plural and singular:
     1. Abbreviations: la **foto**(grafia) > le
         foto
     2. Nouns ending in a consonant:
         il **tram** > i **tram**
     3. Nouns ending in a stressed vowel:
         la **città** > le **città**
 R   Nouns ending in **-i** and **-ie**, for ex.
        la **crisi** (the crisis) > le **crisi**
        la **serie** (the series) > le **serie**

   OP The irregular Plural

EX   The son eats the orange and carrys
       the case.
       Il **figlio** mangia l'**arancia** e porta la
       val**igia** .

21

PL   I figli mangiano le arance e portano
      le valige
D   Nouns ending in **io** (unstressed i):
      Pl **i**
      Nouns ending in **cia** (unstressed i):
      Pl **ce**
      Nouns ending in **gia** (unstressed i):
      Pl **ge**
EX   The drunken pilot is a problem for
      the tourist.
      Il pilota ubriaco è un problema per il
      turista.
Pl   I piloti ubriachi sono un problema
      per i turisti.
D   Masculine nouns ending in **a**: Pl **-i**
      Nouns ending in **ista**: Pl (m) **-isti**
      and (f) **-iste**

      OP Insertion of 'h' to get the hard
          pronunciation
EX   The german and the colleague look at
      the wood and the lake.
      La tedesca e la collega guardano il
      bosco e il lago.
Pl   Le tedesche e le colleghe guardano i
      boschi e i laghi.
D   The words ending in -ca, -ga, -co and
      go have in the plural a **h** in order to
      keep the hard pronunciation.
      Exceptions:
      For ex. l'amico / the friend Pl gli
      amici.

Words ending in - co, - go: when the third-to-last syllable is stressed don't include h in the plural, for example: i medici / the doctors, i psicologi / the psychologists

OP Uses of **ci**

Ci replaces **in** and **a**:
Have you been in Italy? Sei stato **in** Italia?
Non **ci** sono mai stato. There I have never been.
Do you often think of Rome? Pensi spesso **a** Roma?
Sì, **ci** penso spesso. Yes I often think of it.
How do you go to Rome? Come vai **a** Roma?
Ci vado in macchina. There I go by car.
Why are you going to Rome? Perché vai **a** Roma?
C'è qualche amico. There are some friends.

R **Qualche** means some, but is always used in conjunction **with the singular**: qualche giorno / some days
R The word pensare is used in conjunction with **ci**:
Pensa**ci** bene / Think it over well.

OP   Uses oft the Pronominal Adverbe **ne**
Ne replaces phrases with **di**:
Would you like to dance? Hai voglia **di** ballare?

23

Ne ho voglia. I feel like doing that.
How many newspapers do you take? Quanti giornali prendi?
Ne prendo due. I take two of them.
D   Before a verb the part of a quantity is always expressed as **ne**.

<u>Weekdays</u>

Che giorno è oggi?
 Monday lunedì
Tuesday martedì
Wednesday mercoledì
 Thursday giovedì
 Friday venerdì
Saturday sabato
Sunday domenica

<u>Months</u>

January gennaio   September
February febbraio   settembre
March marzo   October
April aprile   ottobre
May   maggio   November
June giugnio   novembre
July luglio   December
August agosto   dicembre

The names of the months and of the week-days are **masculine** (except: **la** domenica).

Please learn the underlined words from <u>cut</u> to <u>flower.</u>

Fourth day

Il guasto all'automobile / The breakdown

Place: Florence
A tourist T, passer-by P, employee E,
mechanic M

T Mi scusi, dov'è l'officina più vicina?
   Excuse me, where is the nearest garage?
P   (ridendo / smiling) Cinque metri dietro
   di Lei. Five meters behind you.
E Buon giorno, cosa c'è? Hello, what is the
   matter?
T   La mia macchina ha un guasto. My car
    has broken dawn. Potrebbe controllare la
   mia macchina? Could you check my car?
   Si è fermata e non riparte. It has just
   stopped and will not start again.
E   Dove si è fermata? Where has it stop-
    ped?
T   Esattamente davanti all'officina. Exactly
   in front of the garage.
E   Bene, è una buona macchina! Well done
   it is a good car! La chiave della macchina, per favore. Please give me the car
   key. Mentre il mio meccanico control-
   lla la machina Lei può bere un caffè.
   While my mechanic checks the car you
   can drink a coffee.
   Il meccanico ritorna dopo cinque minuti.
   The mechanic returns after five minutes.

T Perché la macchina non parte? Why does the car not start?

M Indovini un po'. Have a guess.

T Lo starter non funziona? The starter does not work?

M No.

T La batteria è scarica? Is the battery flat?

M No, ma il serbatoio della benzina è vuoto. No, but the tank is empty.

The Adjective

EX The sympathic boy loves the sympathic girl.
    Il ragazzo simpatico ama la ragazza simpatica. (1)

Pl I ragazzi simpatici amano le ragazze simpatiche. (2)

D Male adjectives on -**o** form the female form on -**a**. (1)

D Adjectives form the **plural as the nouns**. (2)

EX The boy and the girl are sympathic.
    Il ragazzo e la ragazza sono simpatici. (3)

D For nouns of **different gender**, the **male adjectiv**e is used. (3)

R Adjectives **agree in number and gender with the nouns** they accompany.

Position of the adjective

R   In Italian the adjective usually follows the noun.

EX   In an Italian city I have a dear cousin with black hair. This cousin is a beautiful girl, even a very beautiful girl.
In una città **italiana** ho una **cara** cugina coi capelli **neri**. **Quella** cugina è una **bella** ragazza, perfino una ragazza **molto bella**.

D   città **italiana**: Adjectives which express the nationality: after the noun.
cara cugina: short or very common adjectives (nuovo, vecchio, piccolo , grande,lungo, breve) before the noun.
capelli **neri**: the colours after the noun.
quello(a) and bello(a): before the noun.
ragazza **molto bella**: adjectives with an attachment: after the noun.

OP Bello, quello and buono before a noun

EX   The boy and the girl are content after a nice movie or a good concert.
Il ragazzo e la ragazza sono contenti dopo un **bel** film o un **buon** concerto.

bello:
Before a noun bello has the same ending as the definite article:
il film > bel film
quello:
Before a noun quello has the same ending as

the definite article:
il ragazzo > quel ragazzo, i ragazzi > quei
ragazzi, l'albergo > quell'albergo
lo spettacolo > quello spettacolo,
gli spettacoli > quegli spettacoli

buono:
Before a noun (in the Sg) buono has the
same ending as the indefinite article:
un concerto > buon concerto

OP Abbreviation of the Adjective

EX The visit of St. Peter gives me a great
    pleasure.
    La visita di **San** Pietro mi fa una **gran**
    gioia.
R   Saint / Santo: abbreviation **San**; before
    a vowel Sant (Sant' Antonio).
    Great / grande: abbreviation **gran**
    before a vowel grand (grand'amore).

Comparisons of Inequality

A is beautiful / A è **bella**.
B is more beautiful than A / B è **più bella** di
A.
C is the most beautiful / C è **la più bella**.
D is less beautiful than A / D è **meno bella**
di A.
D is the least beautiful / D è **la meno bella**.
D   The comparative of superiority: più +

adjective.

The comparative of inferiority: meno + adjective.

The **superlative** is formed by adding the **definite article before the comparative**.

The Absolute Superlative

Add the suffix -*issimo/a* to the adjective after dropping the final vowel:
bello/a > bell > bell*issimo/a*
Eva è bell*issima*. Eva is very beautiful.

OP The comparative with **di**

EX   Anna è **più** intelligente **di** Eva,
       ma Eva ha il viso più bello.
       Anna is more intelligent than Eva
       but Eva has a more beautiful face.

 R   After the comparative (**più** intelligente)
       for 'than' is used **di**.

OP The comparative with **che**

EX Eva è **più** bella **che** intelligente.
       Il vestito di Eva è **più** lilla **che** blu.
       Eva is more beautiful than intelligent.
       The dress of Eva is more purple than
       blue.

D   When you compare two qualities of the
       same person or thing you must use after
       the comparative the word **che**.

OP Comparisons of Equality

London è **cosi** bella **come** Roma.

London is as beautiful as Rome.
Carlo ha **tanto** denaro **quanto** Luigi.
Carlo has as much money as Luigi.

OP Irregular Comparatives and Superlatives

buono	*migliore*	**il** *migliore*
good	better	the best
cattivo	*peggiore*	**il** *peggiore*
bad	worse	the worst
grande	*maggiore*	**il** *maggiore*
tall	taller	the tallest
piccolo	*minore*	**il** *minore*
small	smaller	the smallest

OP Contrasting Adjectives and Adverbs

old / young **anziano** / **giovane**;   old / new **vecchio** / **nuovo**; outside / inside / **fuori** / **dentro**;   first / last **primo** / **ultimo**;   free / occupied **libero** / **occupato**; early / late **presto** / **tardi**; good / bad **buono** / **cattivo**; big / small **grande** / **piccolo**; hard / soft **duro** / **molle**; light / dark **chiaro** / **scuro**; warm / cold **caldo** / **freddo**;   here / there **qui** / **là**; high / low **alto** / **basso**; up / down **su** / **giù**; behind / in front **dietro** / **davanti**; easy / difficult **facile** / **difficile**; light / heavy **leggero** / **pesante**; long / short **lungo** / **corto**; on the left / on the right **a sinistra** / **a destra**; loud / quiet **rumoroso** / **silenzioso**; near/ distant **vicino** / **lontano**;   up / down

di sopra / **di sotto**; open / closed **aperto** / **chiuso**; right / wrong **giusto** / **sbagliato**; quick / slow **rapido** / **lento**; beautiful / ugly **bello** / **brutto**; strong / weak **forte** / **debole**; sweet / sour **dolce** / **acido**; dry / wet **secco** / **bagnato**; over / under **sopra** / **sotto**; much / few **molto** / **poco**; full / empty **pieno** / **vuoto**; forwards / backwards **avanti** / **indietro**; before / afterwards **prima** / **dopo**.

Introduce yourself and others

Buon giorno. How-do-you-do? Mi chiamo Carlo Visconti. My name is Carlo Visconti. Piacere, il mio nome è Eva Bianco. Very pleased, my name is Eva Bianco.
Buona sera, signor Visconti. Good evening, Mr Visconti. Posso *presentar*La alla signora Celli e al signor Rossi. May I introduce you to Ms Celli and Mr Rossi.

D The definite article is used when talking about a person. He is omitted when addressing a person.

D Titles for men often lose the final vowel before proper names: il signor Rossi, il dottor Manconi, il professor Celli.

Please learn the underlined words from follow to hotel.

31

Fifth day

Primo incontro / First meeting

Piazza del mercato a Capri. Market
square in Capri. Davanti a un albergo.
In front of a hotel. Accanto all'entrata
due valige. Next o the entrance two suit-
cases
una turista / F, un turista M

M   Le piace qui? Do you like it here?
F   Si, mi piace molto. Yes, I like it very
    much.
M   Dove abita? Where do you live?
F   Abito a Roma. I live in Rome.
M   Che sorpresa, anch'io. What a surprise,
    me too.
     Mi chiamo Tino Baci. I am Tino Baci.
F   (sorridendo / smiling) Piacere. Nice to
    see you.
M   Come si chiama? What is your name?
F   Mi chiamo Gina Borelli. I am Gina
    Borelli.
M   Ha trovato un buon albergo? Did you
    find a good hotel?
F   Sì, quel albergo là. Yes, the hotel there.
M   Che sorpresa, anch'io sono in quest'
     albergo. What a surprise, I am also in
    this hotel. È la prima volta che è qui?
    Is this your first time here?

F   Sì, sono qui per la prima volta. Yes it is
    the first time I have been here.
M   È qui con la famiglia? Are you here
    with your family?
F   No, sono sola. No, I am alone.
M   Anch'io. Me too. Sono arrivato ieri. I
    arrived yesterday.   Quando è arrivata?
    When did you arrive?
F   Una settimana fa. A week ago to day.
M   Quanto si ferma? How long are you
    staying?
F   Sto partendo. I am just leaving. Ecco là
    le mie valige. There are my cases.
    Aspetto il taxista per andare al porto. I
    am waiting for the taxi driver in order
    to go to the port.
M   Che peccato! What a pity! Ci possiamo
    incontrare a Roma? Can we meet again
    in Rome? Andiamo al cinema? Would
    you like to go to the cinema?
F   Non mi interesso di cinema. I am not in-
    terested in the cinema.
M   Andiamo in una discoteca? Would you
    like to go to the discotheque?
F   Non voglio andare in discoteca. I do not
    want to go to a discotheque.
M   Di che cosa si occupa nel Suo tempo li-
    bero? What do yo do in your spare ti-
    me?
F   Il mio hobby è l'opera. My hobby is the
    opera.
M   È anche il mio hobby. That is also my

hobby. Ha tempo il sei settembre? Do you have time on the sixth of September?

F   Un attimo, per favore. Just a moment please. Devo vedere nell'agenda. I will have a look in my diary. Sì, quella sera sono libera. Yes, the evening is free.

M   (prende il suo telefonino e compone un numero di telefono / takes his mobile and dials a phone number): Cosa c'è in programma il sei settembre? What is on the sixth of September at the opera? Oh, una première. Oh, a première. Chi è il solista? Who is the soloist? Oh, Placido Domingo. Posso comprare due biglietti? Can I get two tickets? Vorrei prenotare due posti in galleria. I would like to reserve two tickets in the gallery.

F   Cosa danno all'opera? What is on at the opera?

M   'Othello' di Verdi.

Seasons

spring primavera f
autumn autunno m
summer estate f
winter inverno m

The Adverb

EX   The fast boy works fast.
Il ragazzo rapid**o** lavora
*rapida***mente**.

D   Adjectives ending in **o**:
*The feminine form of the adjective
(rapida)* + **mente** >
adverb (*rapida***mente**).

EX   The happy girl smiles happily.
La ragazza felic**e** ride felice**mente**.

D   Adjectives ending in **e**:
Adjective (feli̱ce) + **mente** > adverb
(felice**mente**).

EX   The kind girl greets nicely.
La ragazza gentil**e** saluta
gentil**mente**.

D   Adjectives ending in **le** and **re**:
Adjective without e (gentil) + **mente**
> adverb (gentil**mente**).

R   The adverb is **invariable**.

OP Comparative and Superlative of the Adverb

comparative: *più / meno + adverb.*
superlative: c*omparative* + di tutti/e.
fast / rapidamente, faster / *più rapidamente,*
fastest / *più rapidamente* di tutti/e.

OP Irregular Adverbs

EX   After a good dinner I feel well.
Dopo una bu**o**na cena mi sento bene.

35

D	buono(a) good (adjective)
	bene well (adverbe)
EX	After a bad dinner I feel badly.
	Dopo una cena cattiva mi sento male.
D	cattivo(a) bad (adjective)
	male badly (adverbe)

OP Irregular Comparative Forms

bene	meglio	il meglio
well	better	best
male	peggio	il peggio
badly	worse	worst

OP Similar words

minute	minuto m
moment	momento m
nation	nazione f
person	persona f
philosophy	filosofia f
precious	prezioso
problem	problema m
rose	rosa f
special	speciale
tube	tubo m
use	uso m

Please learn the words from <u>hour</u> to <u>light</u>.

Sixth day

L'abito da sposa / The wedding dress

Luogo: Un negozio di abbigliamento a Roma. A clothing store in Rome.
Gina G, sales assistant / venditrice V

V Posso aiutarLa? Can I help you?
G Sto cercando un abito da sposa. I am looking for a wedding dress.
V Che taglia porta? What size are you?
G Ho la taglia 40. I am size 40.
V Potrebbe descrivermi l'abito che desidera? Could you describe thewedding dress you want to have?
G Desidero un abito elegante. I want to have an elegant dress.
V Di che colore? Which colour?
G Vorrei qualcosa di bianco, però più sul beige che bianco. I want something in white but more beige than white.
V Questo è elegante. This is elegant.
G Posso provarlo? Could I try it on?
V Volentieri. Of course. Ecco le cabine di prova. There are the fitting rooms.
G (sta davanti allo specchio e guarda felice la sua imagine riflessa / stands in front of the mirror and looks happily at her reflection): Mi sta bene. It fits nicely. Che bel abito. What a beautiful dress.

Quest'abito è un sogno. This dress is a dream. Quanto costa questo sogno? How much is this dream?

V   Duemila Euro. Two thousand Euros.

G   Che peccato! What a pity! Non posso spendere più di mille Euro. I cannot pay more than a thousand Euro.

V   Un minuto, per favore. Just a minute please. Telefono al caporeparto. I will speak to the head of department on the phone.

Dopo la telefonata. After the phone call: Può realizzare il sogno con mille cinque cento Euro.You can realize your dream with one thousand and five hundred Euro.

G   Va bene, lo prendo. Okay, I will take it.

OP Irregular Verbs

porre / put
Present: pongo poni pone poniamo ponete pongono
PP: posto

scegliere / select
scelgo scegli sceglie scegliamo scegliete scelgono
PP: scelto

valere / to be worth
valgo vali vale valiamo valete valgono
PP: valso

The three Conjugations

First conjugation: Verbs ending in -**are**
Second conjugation: Verbs ending in-**ere**
Third Conjugation:Verbs ending in -**ire**

endings		conjugation
am-*are*	am-	a̲m-*o* I love
		-*i*
		-a
		-*ia̲mo*
		-a̲te
		a̲m- ano
ve̲nd-*ere*	vend-	ve̲nd-*o* I sell
		-*i*
		-e
		-*ia̲mo*
		-e̲te
		ve̲nd-ono
part-*ire*	part-	pa̲rt-*o* I leave
		-*i*
		-e
		-*ia̲mo*
		-i̲te
		pa̲rt-ono

R The endings of the 1st and 2nd person
   singular and 1st person plural are the
   same for all three conjugations:
   -o, -i, -iamo
   The first vowel of the word ending

determines the first vowel of the 2nd person plural: are > **ate**, ere > **ete**, ire > **ite**

OP <u>Conjugation of the verb capire / understand</u>

cap**isc**-o / I understand	cap-i**a**mo
cap**isc**-i /	cap-i̱te
cap**isc**-e	cap**isc**-ono

Sg and 3. person Pl: Insertion of -**isc** before the ending.

EX If you do not understand how you can clean I prefere that you finish the thing. Se non cap**isc**e, come si pul**isc**e, prefer**isc**o che fin**isc**a la cosa.

R Some verbs have -**isc** before the ending, for example:
capi̱re / understand, puli̱re / clean, preferi̱re / prefer, fini̱re / finish.

OP Verbs ending in -are / -gare have **h** before -i to preserve the hard pronunciation, for example cerc**a**re / look for

cerco I am looking for	cerc**h**iamo
cerc**h**i	cerc**a**te
cerca	ce̱rcano

OP Imperfect, Future, Conditional

Imperfect	am-	**av**	ama**v**o	I loved
	vend-	**ev**	vende**v**o	I sold
	part-	**iv**	part**iv**-o	I leaved
			-**i**	
			-**a**	
			-**amo**	
			-**ate**	
		part**iv**	-**ano**	

Future	am-	**e**	am**er**ò	I will love
	vend-	**e**	vend**er**ò	I will sell
	part-	**i**	parti-**rò**	I will leave
			-**rai**	
			-**rà**	
			-**remo**	
			-**rete**	
			-**ranno**	

Conditional	am-	**e**	am**er**ei	I would love
	vend-	**e**	vend**er**ei	I would sell
	part-	**i**	parti-**rei**	I would leave
			-**resti**	
			-**rebbe**	
			-**remmo**	
			-**reste**	
			-**rebbero**	

With the conditional mood one can formulate a question or a request:

Mi sap**r**ebbe dire che ore sono?

Could you tell me what time it is?

In addition, one can express a wish:

Vivr**e**i volenti**e**ri a Roma. I would like to live
in Rome.

R Formation of the perfect:
   Presence of auxiliary verbs **have** / avere
   or **be** / essere + **past participle (PP)** of
   the verb.
The past participle is formed by dropping
the infinitive ending -are, -ere, -ire and
adding -ato (first conjugation), -uto (second
conjugation) and -ito (third conjugation).

am-	**ato**	ho am**ato**	I have loved
vend-	**uto**	ho vend**uto**	I have sold
part-	**ito**	sono part**ito**	I have leaved

OP <u>Past Participle conjugated with essere</u>
EX   The boy has teturned. The girl has
     returned.
     Il ragazzo è ritorn**ato**. La ragazza è
     ritorn**ata**.
Pl   I ragazzi sono ritorn**ati**. Le ragazze
     sono ritorn**ate**.
D **The past participle conjugated with**
   essere agrees in gender and number
   with the subject of the verb.
R   The following verbs use the past
    participle with essere:
    Reflexive verbs (Mi sono informato / I

have informed myself)
Some verbs which express a movement, for example:
andare / to go, arrivare / to arrive, partire / to start.

OP Past Participle conjugated with avere

EX   The boy / the girl has made a phone call.
　　Il ragazzo / la ragazza ha telefon<u>a</u>t**o.**
Pl   I ragazzi / Le ragazze hanno telefon<u>a</u>t**o.**
D   The past participle conjugated with avere remains **invariable.**

Exception: The past participle agrees in gender and number with the proceeding direct object.

EX   Did you see the boy / the girl? I have seen him
　　Ha visto il ragazzo? **L'**ho vist**o.**
　　Ha visto la ragazza? **L'**ho vist**a.**
PL   Ha visto i ragazzi? Li ho vist**i.**
　　Ha visto le ragazze? Le ho vist**e.**
D   Before h and vowel: lo, la > **l'.**

OP Irregular Past Participle

EX I <u>was</u> in the auther's reading and <u>saw</u> the following: The auther <u>opened</u> the book and <u>said</u>: I have <u>made</u> this book, which I have <u>written</u> and <u>read</u> from, a bestseller so that you will remember me after I <u>die</u>.

R   Some verbs have an irregular past
     participle, for example:
     be: essere / **stato**, see: vedere / **visto**,
     open: aprire / **aperto**, say: dire / **detto**,
     make: fare / **fatto** write: scrivere /
     scritto, read: leggere / **letto** die:
     morire / **morto**.

OP The Present Participle and the Imperative

The present participle is formed by dropping
the infinitive ending -are, -ere, -ire and adding -ando (1. conjugation) and -endo (2.
and 3. conjugation).

amare	am- **ando**	am**ando**	loving
vendere	vend- **endo**	vend**endo**	selling
partire	part- **endo**	part**endo**	leaving

Imperative: if you use the polite form of
address to sb: The Imperative is formed by
dropping the infinitive ending and adding
-i (1.conjugation) and a (2.+3.conjugation).

scusare	scus- **i**	scus**i**	excuse
vendere	vend- **a**	vend**a**	sell
partire	part- **a**	part**a**	leave

Imperative: if you are on familiar terms with
sb: The Imperative is formed by dropping
the infinitive ending and adding -a (1. conjugation) and -i (2.+3. conjugation).

44

scus<u>a</u>re	scus-	**a**		scus<u>a</u>	excuse
v<u>e</u>ndere	vend-	**i**		vend**i**	sell
part<u>i</u>re	part-	**i**		part**i**	leave

In the imperative of the 2nd person singular,
in case of negation, the infinitive is used:
non v<u>e</u>ndere / do not sell

Irregular verbs

and<u>a</u>re / to go
Present: vado, vai, va, andiamo, andate,
vanno
PP: andato
fare / to make
Present: faccio, fai, fa, facciamo, fate, fanno
PP: fatto
pot<u>e</u>re / to can
Present: posso, puoi, può, possiamo, potete,
possono
PP: potuto
vol<u>e</u>re / to want
Present: voglio, vuoi, vuole, vogliamo,
volete, vogliono
PP: voluto
ven<u>i</u>re to come
Present: vengo, vieni, viene, veniamo,
venite, vengono
PP: venuto

**Please learn the words from <u>liqueur</u> to
<u>party</u>.**

Seventh day

Il viaggio di nozze / The honeymoon

Luogo: L'aeroporto di Roma-Ciampino.
Place: The airport Ciampino in Rome.
Gina G, Tino T, employee E

T   Quando parte il volo charter per Parigi?
When does the charter plane leave for
Paris?

E   Avete ancora un po'di tempo. You have
still a little time. Non parte prima delle
nove. The plane does not take off until
nine o'clock.

G   A che ora arriva l'aereo a Parigi? What
time does the plane get at Paris?

E   Se l'aereo parte in orario, l'arrivo è alle
undici. If the plane takes off on time the
arrival is at eleven o'clock.

E   È la prima volta che andate a Parigi?
Are you going to Paris for the first time?

G   Sì, è il nostro viaggio di nozze. Yes, it is
our honeymoon.

E   Felicitazioni agli sposi. Congratulations
on your marriage. Avete trovato un
buon albergo? Did you find a good hotel?

T   Sì, vicino alla cattedrale *Notre-Dame*
nel *Quartier Latin.*Yes, nearby the cathedral *Notre-Dame* in the *Quartier*

latin.

E   Sono vissuto in questo quartiere dal
1988 al 1996. I lived in this districct of
Paris from 1988 to 1996. Ogni volta che
penso a Parigi, sento una grande nos-
talgia di quella città meravigliosa. Each
time when I remember Paris I am
homesick for that wonderful city.

G   Che cosa Le è piaciuto più di tutto a
Parigi? What impressed you most in
Paris?

E   È una domanda difficile. It is a difficult
question. Forse la vista sulla *Senna*
sotto i ponti di Parigi oppure la vista
dal mio appartamento sul cielo azzurro
sopra i tetti di Parigi. Perhaps the view
of the Seine under the bridges of Paris
or the view from my apartment of the
blue sky over the roofs of Paris. Forse
quella sera sulla piazza *Concorde*
mentre il sole rosso tramontava dietro
alla torre Eiffel. Perhaps that evening on
place Concorde when the red sun was
setting behind the Eiffel tower. Forse
quella notte, quando ho guardato il mare
di luce della città dal ristorante più alto
della torre Eiffel. Perhaps that night,
when I looked at the light of the city
from the highest restaurant of the Eiffel
tower. Forse la bellezza seducente delle
ballerine del *Lido* e del *Moulin Rouge.*
Perhaps the seductive beauty of the dan-

cers in the *Lido* and the *Moulin Rouge*.
Forse la mattina in cui ho visto davanti alla
chiesa *Sacré-Coeur* dopo una notte in
bianco il sorgere del sole roseo. Perhaps that
morning after a sleepless night in front of
the church *Sacré-Coeur* when I looked at the
rosy light of the sunrise. Che cosa mi è
piaciuto più di tutto? What impressed me
most? Non lo so. I don't know. Ma so che
sarete molto felici tutti e due durante questo
viaggio di nozze perché Parigi è la città
perfetta per amarsi e perciò il luogo ideale
per un viaggio di nozze. But I know, that
you will be very happy during your
honeymoon because Paris is the perfect city
for love and therefore the ideal place for a
honeymoon. Per quanto tempo vi fermate a
Parigi? How long will you stay in Paris?

T   Due settimane. Two weeks.

G   Forse anche qualche giorno in più. Per-
      haps also some days moreover.

E   Saluti Parigi da parte mia. Say hello to
      Paris for me. Buon volo e buona luna di
      miele! Have a good flight and a happy
      honeymoon!

OP Irregular Verbs

vedere / see
Present: vedo vedi vede vediamo vedete
vedono
PP: visto

The Reflexive Pronoun

mi lavo / I wash myself   ci laviamo
ti lavi   vi lavate
si lava   **si** lavano

The Personal Pronouns: unstressed

The Direct Object Pronoun (DOP)

R   The direct object pronoun can be derived from the reflexive pronouns by replacing si (Sg) with **lo** (him) and **la** (her) and si (Pl) with **li** (them m) and **le** (them f): mi, ti, **lo**, **la**, ci, vi **li**, **le**

EX   I love *you* / io *ti* amo

subject pronoun	DOP	verb
io (I)	ti (you)	amo
tu (you)	mi (me)	ami
lui (he)	**la** (her) **La** (m w)	ama
lei (she) **Lei** (m w)	**lo** (him)	ama
noi (we)	vi (you)	amiamo
voi (you)	ci (us)	amate
loro (they m)	**le** (them w) **Le** (w)	amano
loro (they f)	**li** (them m) **Li** (m)	amano

Lei (nominative): Where are you from, my lady/sir?
Lei di dov'è, Signora/e? Pl **Loro** di dove sono, Signore/i?
La (accusative): I greet you, my lady/sir. **La** saluto, Signora/e. Pl **Le** saluto, Signore. **Li**

saluto, Signor**i**.

R 'Thank' and 'help' stand with accusative:
Can I help you? **La** posso aiutare? Thank
you. **La** ringrazio.

EX **I** take a dessert and you?
   Io prendo un dess<u>e</u>rt e **tu**?
R **The subject pronoun is used in order to
   highlight a person (io) or if it is placed
   alone (e tu?).**

The Indirect Object Pronouns (IOP)

R   The indirect object pronouns can be
derived from the reflexive pronouns by
replacing si (Sg) with **le** (her) **gli** (him) and
si (Pl) with **loro** (them): mi, ti, **le**, **gli**, ci, vi,
loro

EX I sell you a coffee / Io *ti* vendo un caffè

Subject pronoun	IOP	Verb
io (I)	ti (you)	vendo
tu (you)	mi (me)	vendi
lui (he)	**le** (her) **Le**	vende
lei (she)	**gli** (him)	vende
noi (we)	vi (you)**Vi**	vendi<u>a</u>mo
voi (you)	ci (us)	vend<u>e</u>te
loro (they)	**loro** (them)	vendono
		v<u>e</u>ndono loro un caffè

EX Does the cake taste good, my lady /
   sir? **Le** piace la torta, Signora/e?
EX I write to you, ladies / gentlemen.

50

Vi scrivo, Signore/i.
I tell you, ladies / gentlemen.
Dico **Loro**, Signore/i.

R   **Loro** and **loro**: always after the verb.
EX   I sell it to **you**. **Te** *lo* vendo. (1)
R   Rules when two pronouns meet:
     Mi, ti, ci, vi, si become me, te, ce, ve,
     se.
D   The indirect pronoun is placed before
     the direct pronoun. (1)

R   **gli** + *lo*, *li*, *la*, *le* become **glie***lo*, **glie***li*,
     glie*la*, **glie***le*.
EX   Show the room to Mr. X. Mostri la
     camera al signore X.. I show it to
     him. **Glie***la* mostro.

Stressed Forms of the Personal Pronouns

EX I'am leaving with you / io parto con **te**.

stressed subject pronoun	verb	pronoun
io	parto	con **te** (with you)
tu	parti	con **me** (with me)
lui	parte	con lei (with her)
lei	parte	con lui (with him)
noi	partiamo	con voi (with you)
voi	partite	con noi (with us)
loro	partono	con loro (with them)

R The stressed pronouns can be derived
   from the subject pronouns by replacing io

and tu with **me** and **te**:
me, te, lui, lei, noi, voi, loro

R   **The personal pronouns are stressed after the prepositions**: for me / per **me**
The personal pronouns are stressed, when they serve to highlight a person: Carlo loves **you** / Carlo ama **te**.

OP <u>The Personal Pronoun: two constructions</u>

EX   Eva knows *me* / Eva *mi* conosce.
D   The pronoun (*mi*) is placed before the verb (conosce).
R   If the sentence contains a conjugated verb and an infinitive, there are **two possibilities for the position of the pronoun**.
EX   I want to inform myself.
Mi vorrei informare. Vorrei informar-*mi*.
R   If the personal pronoun is hung on the infinitive, the 'e' of the infinitive is omitted.

Please learn the words from <u>pay</u> to <u>shoe</u>.

Eighth day

Arrivo all'albergo / Arrival at the hotel

Un albergo a San Remo. A hotel in San Remo.
Tino T, sua moglie Gina G, la loro figlia Nora N, il signor Ricci R

T Buona sera, il mio nome è Tino Baci. Good evening, my name is Tino Baci. Lei è il signor Ricci a cui ho telefonato la settimana scorsa? Are you Mr Richard to whom I spoke on the phone last week?

R Sì, lieto di conoscervi. Yes, pleased to meet you. Quanto vi fermate? How long are you staying?

T Una settimana. One week. Abbiamo bisogno di una camera doppia e di una camera singola per nostra figlia. We need a double room and a single room for our daughter.

R Avete fortuna. You are lucky. Benché siamo in alta stagione ci sono ancora alcune camere libere. Although it is the high season there are still some free rooms. Ci sono due camere con bagno, balcone e vista sul mare. There are two rooms overlooking the see with a bathroom and a balcony.

G Quanto costano con la colazione, la

mezza pensione e la pensione completa?
How much is it with breakfast, half board
and full board?

R Ecco la lista dei prezzi. This is the price
list.

G È troppo caro. That is too expensive. Ha
qualcosa di più conveniente? Do you
have anything cheaper?

R Sì, abbiamo due camere con doccia e
vista sulle montagne. Yes, we have two
rooms overlooking the mountains and
with shower.

G Possiamo vedere le camere? Can we see
the rooms?

R Volentieri. Of course.
Dopo la visita. After the viewing.

G Va bene, prendiamo le camere. Okay, we
will take the rooms.

R Per favore compili questo modulo di
iscrizione. Would you fill out this appli-
cation form. Firmi qui, per cortesia.
Would you sign please here.

T Qualcuno potrebbe portare su i bagagli?
Could somebody take the luggage up?

R Chiamo un cameriere. I will call for a
servant. Ecco tutte e due le chiavi. These
are the two keys.

G A che ora è la colazione? What time is
breakfast?

R Dalle otto alle dieci. From eight till ten.

T Potrebbe svegliarci domattina alle otto?
Could you wake us at eight tomorrow

54

morning?

R Volentieri. Of course. Ecco l'ascensore. There is the lift. Buona notte. Good night. A domani. See you tomorrow.

Dopo una settimana bellissima. After a very good week.

T Mi prepari il conto, per favore. Can you do the bill for me.

R Il conto è pronto. The bill is ready.

T Arrivederci, siamo stati molto bene. Goodbye, it was very nice.

G È stata una settimana meravigliosa. It was a wonderful week.

N Ciao, è stato mega fantastico. Bye, it was mega fantastic.

R Piacere di avervi conosciuti. It was nice meeting you. Spero di rivedervi l'anno prossimo. I hope to see you again next year. Buon ritorno. Have a good journey home.

The Demonstrative Pronoun

EX Which girl is more beautiful: this or that? Quale ragazza è più bella: questa o quella?

object	near	further away
Sg	**questo/a** è …	**quello/a** è
Pl	**questi/e** sono …	**quelli/e** sono

R The use oft he demonstrative pronoun is determined **by the distance**.

R The **gender** and **number** of the demonstrative pronoun is determined **by the**

corresponding noun.

Possessive Adjectives and Pronouns

adjectives	pronouns
EX My garage, etc.	Mine, etc.
.	
il mio garage	**il** mio
il tuo garage	**il** tuo
il suo garage	**il** suo
il nostro garage	**il** nostro
il vostro garage	**il** vostro
il loro garage	**il** loro

R   Before the possessive adjectives and
     pronouns is always placed the definite
     article.
     Exception: family members in the Sg.

EX **One contact**: When does your friend
     arrive?
Sg: Quando viene **il Suo** amico / **la Sua**
     amica?
Pl: Quando vengono **i Suoi** amici / **le
     Sue** amiche?
     Several contacts:
Sg: Quando viene **il Vostro** amico / **la
     Vostra** amica?
Pl: Quando vengono **i Vostri** amici / **le
     Vostre** amiche?
EX I see first your friend, then his brother

and his sisters.
Vedo prima **il tuo** amico, dopo **suo**
fratello e **le sue** sorelle.
I see first your girlfriend, then her
sister and her brothers.
Vedo prima **la tua** amica, dopo **sua**
sorella e **i suoi** fratelli.
I see your friends first, then their
brothers and sisters.
Vedo prima **i tuoi** amici, dopo **i loro**
fratelli e **le loro** sorelle.

R   The possessive pronoun **loro** is always
used with the definite article and is
invariable.

EX Carlo parked **his** car. Carlo ha parcheg-
giato **la sua** macchina.(**f**)
Eva parked **her** car. Eva ha parcheg-
giato **la sua** macchina.(**f**)

D   The gender oft he possessive pronoun
depends on the **gender oft the property**.

OP The Relative Pronouns

Hermann Hesse who is a Nobel prize
winner, who everyone knows, reads two
poems which I know and which are my
favourite poems.

Hermann Hesse **che** (1) è un premio Nobel,
che (2) molte persone conoscono, legge due
poesie **che** (3) conosco e **che** (4) sono le mie
poesie preferite.

The relative pronoun **che** is used for masculine words (1), feminine words (3), persons

57

(1,2), things (3,4) singular (1,2), plural (3,4) nominative (1+4), accusative (2+3).
After a preposition che > cui:
Eva e Carlo a **cui** ho telefonato. Eva and Carlo, with who I have made a call.

OP Essential expressions and questions

I would like to / vorrei get off / scendere, take away / portare via, visit / visitare, pay / pagare, make an appointment / fissare un appuntamento, deposit in the safe / depositare nella cassaforte.
Do I need to / devo reserve / prenotare, change / cambiare?
Can I / posso park here / parcheggiare qui, leave the luggage here / lasciare il bagaglio qui, take pictures / è permesso fare delle foto, walk / andare a piedi, invite you / La invitare, acompany you home / La accompagnare a casa?
Can you / può bring me / portarmi, give me / darmi, recommend me / raccomandarmi, explain me / spiegarmi, help me / aiutarmi, borrow me / noleggiarmi, get me / procurarmi, show me / mostrarmi, call me a taxi / chiamarmi un taxi?
Who / chi is the tour guide / è la guida turistica? **Whom / a chi** can I contact / mi posso rivolgere? **Who / di chi** is this jacket from / è questa giacca? **With whom / con**

chi do you go out / esci?

Who / da chi have you been to / sei stato?

What / che, che cosa, cosa is there / che c'è, is that / che cos'è, is new / cosa c'è di nuovo, do you do for a living / che lavoro fa, did you talk about / di che ha parlato / are you thinking / a che cosa pensi, is the weather forecast / come sono le previsioni del tempo, time is it / che ore sono, charge per day / qual' è la tariffa giornaliera, voltage / qual' è il voltaggio?

When / quando starts / inizia, is admission / l'entrata è dalle che ore, does it open (close) / apre (chiude), will leave (arrive) parte (arriva), is the next … / è il / la proximo(a)…? **Since when / da quando** are you here / sei qui?

Where / dove can I find (buy) / posso trovare (comprare), do you by the tickets / si comprano i biglietti, does it take place / a luogo / is this train going / va questo treno?

Where is the / dov'è next gas station / il distributore più vicino, car rental / l'auto-noleggio, luggage storage / il deposito bagagli, ticket office / la biglietteria, check-in counter / il banco del check-in, cash machine / il Bancomat, tourist office / l'ufficio per il turismo, mailbox / la cassetta delle lettere, police / la polizia?

How / come are you / sta Lei, do I get to / posso andare a, far is it to … / quanto dista long does it take / quanto tempo dura?

How much / **quanto** is … per hour / costa
… all'ora?

Which / **qual' è …** tephone number / il
numero di telefono, area code / il prefisso,
address / l'indirizzo?

The interrogative sentence

The interrogative sentence is formed by
stressing **the end of the sentence**, f. ex.
Eva parla inglese / Eva speaks English.
Eva parla **inglese** / Does Eva speak English?

OP Irregular verbs

dovere / to have to
present: devo, devi deve, dobbiamo, dovete,
devono
PP: dovuto
dire / to say
present: dico, dici, dice, diciamo, dite,
dicono
PP: detto
dare / to give
present: do, dai, dà, diamo, date, danno
PP: dato

Negatives

R   The negative is expressed with the words **no** and **non**. Non is placed before the verb / *pronoun* / **auxiliary verb**:

EX   I do not see R. Non vedo R. I do not see him. Non *lo* vedo. I did not see R. Non **ho** visto R.

R   The negation can also be expressed by two negative parts (double negation).

EX   I do not see R. anymore. **Non** vedo **più** R.

I never see R. **Non** vedo **mai** R.

I do not see R. nor S. **Non** vedo **né** R. **né** S.

I do not see anyone. **Non** vedo **nessuno**.

I see nothing. **Non** vedo **niente**.

R   With emphasis, the strong negative part is placed at the beginning of the sentence, the weak negative part is omitted: Nobody came. **Nessuno** è venuto.

OP The verb andare / to go and prepositions

EX   I go to Claudia; we go by car to Switzerland and after it to Rome, where we go in a pizzeria and after it we go sleep.

Vado **da** Claudia; andiamo **in** macchina **in** Svizzera e dopo **a** Roma, dove andiamo **in** pizzeria e poi andiamo **a** dormire.

D   **da** Claudia: persons: and<u>a</u>re **da**
     in macchina: means of transport:
     andare **in**
     in Svizzera: country: andare **in**
     a Roma: town: andare **a**
     in pizzeria: shop with ending -ia:
     andare **in**
     andiamo **a** dormire: between andare
     and infinitive: **a**

OP <u>The pronoun 'si'</u>

EX When you are ill you can take different
     medicaments.
     Quando si è mal<u>a</u>ti**,** si p<u>o</u>ssono assu-
     mere div<u>e</u>rse medic<u>i</u>ne.
D   In the case of the combination of si +
     essere + adjective:
     the adjective is always ending in -**i.**
     After si the verb is in the plural (si
     p<u>o</u>ssono)**, if the noun to which it re-**
     fers (medic<u>i</u>ne) **is in the plural.**
EX You often see each other.
     Ci si vede spesso.
D   si / one becomes before si: **ci**

Please learn the words from <u>shop</u> to <u>table</u>.

Ninth day

Al ristorante / In the restaurant

Gina G, Tino T, Nora N, waitress W

T   Buon giorno. Good morning. Ci scusi, siamo in ritardo. Sorry, we are late.

W Non si preoccupi. Do not worry about it.

T   Il mio nome è Tino Baci. My name is Tino Baci. Ho prenotato un tavolo per tre persone nel settore non fumatori. I have booked a table for three in the non smoking area.

W Ecco il tavolo. Here is your table. Prego si accomodi. Please take a seat. Ecco un menù e la lista delle bevande.Here are a menu and the drink list. Desiderate un aperitivo? Would you like an aperitif?

G Un campari liscio. A pure Campari.

N Un aperitivo analcolico. An alcohol-free aperitif.

T   Un campari con ghiaccio. A campari with ice cubes.
    Dopo l'aperitivo. After the aperitif.

W Che cosa desiderate da bere? What would you like to drink?

G Un bicchiere di vino bianco. A glass of white wine.

N Un succo di frutta. A fruit juice.

T   Una birra alla spina. A draught beer.

W   Cosa desiderate come antipasto? What

would you like as a starter?

T Una zuppa di verdura. A vegetable soup.

G Insalata di pasta. Pasta salad.

N Prosciutto e melone. Ham and melon.

W Che cosa desiderate mangiare? What would you like to eat?

N Prendo un piatto vegetariano. I will have a vegetarian dish. Che cosa mi consiglia? What do you recommend?

W Sogliola con contorno di riso. Sole and rice as side dish.

T Vorrei del pesce. I want fish.

G Prendo bistecca e insalata mista. I will have the beefsteak and mixed salad.

W Che condimento per l'insalata? What kind of dressing would you like?

G Condimento italiano. Italian dressing.

W La bistecca al sangue, a puntino o ben cotta? The steak rare, medium or well done?

G A puntino. Medium.
Dopo il piatto principale. After the main course.

W Desiderate un dessert? Do you like a dessert?

T Macedonia e un pasticcino e una tazza di tè con limone. Fruit salad and pastry and a cup of tea with lemon.

N Che gusti di gelato ci sono? What kind of ice cream do you have?

W Vaniglia,lampone, fragola, noce e albi- cocca. Vanilla, rasberies, strawberries, walnut and apricot.

N Un gelato misto e un caffelatte. A mixed ice cream and a coffee with milk.

G Che torte ci sono? What kind of cake do you have?

W Dolce di frutta, torta di mele e torta di ricotta. Fruitcake, apple cake and cheese cake.

G Una torta di mele ma per favore con panna montata, e un espresso. An apple cake but please with whipped cream and an espresso.

Dopo un pranzo molto buono. After an excellent lunch.

W Vi è piaciuto? Did you enjoy it?

G Era tutto eccellente. It was excellent. Faccia i nostri complimenti allo chef. Would you give our compliments to the chef.

T Il conto per favore. May I have the bill please? Un conto unico. All together. Il resto mancia. Keep the change.

W Grazie. Thank you.

OP The space / lo spazio

in the house	in casa
inside …	all'interno della casa
outside …	fuori della casa
in front of …	davanti alla casa
behind …	dietro la casa
beside …	accanto alla casa
nearby …	vicino alla casa

OP The arrival / l'arrivo

I arrived ...	**Sono arrivato** …
last week …	la settimana scorsa
three days ago	tre giorni fa
the day before yesterday	l'altro ieri
yesterday	ieri
today	oggi
a little while ago	poco tempo fa
half an hour ago	mezz'ora fa
I have just arrived	sono appena arrivato
I am just arriving	sto *arrivando*

If you want to express that something is just happening:
use stare + *Present Participle.*

OP The departure / la partenza

I am going to leave	sto per *partire*

For an imminent action one uses stare per + *infinitive.*

I leave …	**parto** …
immediately	subito
soon	presto
as soon as possible	al più presto
in two hours	fra due ore
this morning	stamattina
this afternoon	oggi pomeriggio
this evening	stasera
this night	stanotte
tomorrow	domani
the day after tomorrow	dopodomani

OP Frequency

never	mai
practically never	quasi mai
now and then	ogni tanto
some times	talvolta
often	spesso
mostly	per lo più
always	sempre

If you haven't understand

I did not understand. Non ho capito. Could you repeat it and speak more slouly. Può ripetere e parlare più lentamente. Can you write it down for me? Me lo può scrivere? Could you translate that for me? Potrebbe tradurre questo per me? What is that in Italian? Come si dice in italiano? What does that mean? Che significa questo? How do you pronounce this word? Come si pronuncia questa parola?

OP In the supermarket

Is there a department store round here? Ci sono dei grandi magazzini qui vicino? I am looking for … Sto cercando …Whom should I speak to? A chi devo rivolgermi? **Posso aiutarLa? Can I help you?** I am just looking, thanks. Grazie, vorrei solo dare un'occhiata.

How much is that? Quanto costa questo?

That is to expensive. È troppo caro. Do you

have anything cheaper? Ha qualcosa di più conveniente? I like that; I will take it. Mi piace questo; lo prendo. Can I pay with this credit card? Posso pagare con questa carta di credito? Could you give me a receipt? Potrebbe rilasciarmi una ricevuta? Could you give me a bag? Potrebbe darmi un saccetto?

OP After an accident

There has been an accident. C'è stato un incidente. Two people have been hurt. Due persone sono ferite. Call an ambulance and the police, quick. Chiami un'ambulanza e la polizia, presto. Could you give me your name, your address and your insurance number? Per favore mi dia il suo nome, il suo indirizzo e il nome della sua assicurazione.

OP Irregular Verbs

sedere / sit
Present: siedo siedi siede sediamo sedete
siedono   PP: seduto
uscire / go out
esco esci esce usciamo uscite escono
PP: uscito
piacere / please
piaccio piacci piacce piacciamo piaccete
piacciono PP: piaciuto

Please learn the words from <u>take</u> to <u>yesterday</u>.

Tenth day

Prepositions of time

4 months ago I hit on the idea of writing a book which I have written since 2 months which I have to finish in 2 months and which the editor publishes in 4 months.

4 mesi **fa** (1) mi è venuto in mente di scrivere un libro che scrivo **da** due mesi (2) che devo terminare **in** 2 mesi (3) e che l'editore pubblica **fra** 4 mesi (4).

D 4 mesi **fa**: time in the past (1).

da 2 mesi: an unfinished action which has begun in the past (2).

in 2 mesi: necessary time for the finishing of an action (3).

fra 4 mesi: time in the future (4).

a

You have to go home on foot because you have to be at home at midnight.

Bisogna andare **a** casa (1) **a** piedi (2) perché bisogna essere **a** casa (3) **a** mezzanotte (4).

a indicates: direction (1), means (2) place (3), time (4).

da

Claudia came from Rome. Claudia è venuta **da** Roma (1).

69

Since yesterday she lives with a friend she is loved by. **Da** ieri (2) abita **da** un amico (3), **da** cui è amata (4). She will stay from 1 to 8 August. Resta **dall'**1 agosto **al** 8 agosto (5). **da** is used, for example, for a starting point of movement (1), for the words 'since' (2) 'with' (3) by (4), times with from ... to (5).

di

Claudia's father often talks about music. Il padre di Claudia parla spesso **di** musica (1). He is from Rome. È nativo **di** Roma (2). **di** is used, for example, for the words 'about' (1), from' (2).

in

My sister lives in France. Mia sorella abita **in** Francia (1). In summer she travels by train to Italy. **In** estate (2) va **in** treno (3) **in** Italia (4). **in** is used, for example, for the word ,in' (1), for times (2), for means of transport (3), for the word 'to' (4).

per

I am going to Rome for love in order to visit my girlfriend. Parto **per** Roma (1) **per** amore (2) **per** (3) visitare la mia amica. I drive trough Florence through Tuscany. Passo **per**

Firenze (4) **per** la Toscana (4). My girlfriend
eats vegetarian food instead of meat because
of her love for the animals. La mia amica
mangia alimentari vegetariani **per** carne (5)
per il suo amore (6) **per** gli animali (2).
Per is used, for example, for the words 'to'
(1), for' (2), in order to (3), ' through' (4),
'instead of' (5), 'because of' (6).

OP Irregular verbs

salire get in
Present: salgo, sali, sale, saliamo, salite,
salgono
PP: salito
tenere   hold
Present: tengo, tieni, tiene, teniamo, tenete,
tengono.
PP: tenuto
stare: stay, be, stand
Present: sto, stai, sta, stiamo state, stanno
PP: stato
sapere: to know
Present: so, sai, sa, sappiamo, sapete, sanno
PP: saputo

OP <u>Quando si è malati … When you are ill</u>

There is a doctor / a pharmacy around here?
C'è una farmacia / un dottore qui vicino?

I am …	**Sono** …
allergic to	allergico a
vaccinated against	vaccinato contro
I have faint	svenuto
I have had a fall	caduto
… months pregnant	incinta di … mesi
diabetic	diabetico(a)

I have …	**Ho** …
a headache	il mal di testa
an earache	il mal d'orecchie
a soer throat	il mal di gola
backache	il mal di schiena
got an upset stomach	il mal di stomaco
stomachache	il mal di pancia
a cold	un raffredore
a temperature	la febbre
a cough	la tosse
an indigestion	un'indigestione
diarrhoea	la diarrea
been sick	vomitato
high/low blood pressure	la pressione alta / bassa
a stiff neck	il torcicollo
circulatory trouble	i disturbi circolatori
it hurts here	ho dei dolori qui

I take this medication regularly. Prendo queste medicine regularmente.

OP Il casino / The casino

Il signor Müller è un giocatore appassionato.
Mr. Müller is a passionate gambler. Per
questo chiama un taxi davanti alla stazione
di Napoli e dice al taxista:
    "Al casino per favore."
Therefore he calls a taxi in front of the station of Naples and says to the driver:
    ‚Al casino, per favore.‘
Dopo 5 minuti il taxista dice con una
strizzatina d'occhi:
    "Ecco l'entrata del casino."
After 5 minutes the driver says with a wink:
    "There is the entrance to the casino."
Alla ricezione siede una bella signora che
saluta il signor Müller con un sorriso gentile.
At the reception sit's a beautiful lady, who
greets Mr. Müller with a friendly smile.

    "Scusi", dice il signor Müller, "il dogani-
ere a detto che il mio passaporto è scaduto."

    "Excuse me", says Mr. Müller, "the cus-
toms officer said, that my passport has expired."

    "Qui non ha bisogno del passaporto; i no-
stri clienti tengono all'anonimità", dice la
donna con una strizzatina d'occhi.

    "Here your passport isn't necessary; our
clients set great store by anonymity", says
the lady with a wink.

    "Molto gentile da parte sua. In Germania
si deve mostrare ogni volta il passaporto se

si va in un casino."

"That's really kind of you. In Ger many you must produce your passport every time you go to casino."

"In questo momento tutte le stanze sono occupate; ma può bere un aperitivo al bar a spese del casino."

"At the moment all the rooms are occupied but you can drink an aperitif in the bar at the expence of the casino."

Il professor Müller guarda con grande stupore il profondo decolleté della barista dal seno pieno che dice con un sorriso seducente:

"Cosa desidera?"

Mr. Müller looks with great astonishment at the deep décolletage of the full-bosomed bar maid, who says with a smile:

"What would you like?"

Siccome è molto caldo nel casino, risponde:

"Un aperitivo con ghiaccio."

Because it's very hot, he answers:

"A campari with ice"

La barista domanda:

"Lei di dov'è?"

The barmaid asks:

"Where do you come from?"

"Sono di un piccolo villagio vicino a Baden-Baden in Germania."

"I come from a little village near Baden-Baden in Germany."

"Che lavoro fa? What do you do for a living?"

"Sono un insegnante di tedesco. I am a German teacher."

La strizzatina d'occhi della barista ricorda al signor Müller la strizzatina d'occhi del taxista e della signora alla ricezione. The winking of the barmaid reminds Mr. Müller of the winking of the driver and the lady at the reception.

"È la Sua prima volta in un casino?"

"Are you in a casino for the first time?"

"No, a Baden-Baden vado al casino due volte la settimana, per lo più tutta la notte; una volta che ho iniziato non posso più smettere."

"No, in Baden-Baden I go to the casino twice a week, mostly the whole night. When I have begun I cannot stop."

"Quando è stato la prima volta in un casino?"

"When did you go to a casino for the first time?"

"Trent'anni fa abbiamo fatto il viaggio di nozze a Monte - Carlo. Thirty years ago we spent our honeymonn in Monte-Carlo. Mentre mia moglie faceva acquisti, sono andato al casino. While my wife went shopping I went to the casino. L'importo minimo era basso; quanto è qui l'importo minimo? The minimum stake was very low; what is the minimum stake here?"

"Due cento Euro. Two hundred Euro"

"Oh, come è alto! Oh, it's very high! A

Baden-Baden l'importo minimo è solo due Euro. In Baden - Baden the minimum stake is only two Euro."

Improvvisamente si apre una porta. Suddenly a door opens. Un uomo appare e dietro di cui il signor Müller vede una ragazza bionda, vestita solo con uno slip rosso. A gentleman comes out and behind him Mr. Müller sees a blond girl dressed only in some pink pants. Ora capisce dove si trova e che significato ha la strizzatina d'occhi ripetuta tre volte. Now he understands, where he is and the meaning of the three winks. Poi inizia a dire parolacce. Then he begins to get angry.:

"Che taxista stupido! What a stupid driver! Ho detto 'al casino, per favore'! I said 'al casino, per favore'!"

La barista ride. The barmaid laughs:

"Non rimproveri il taxista. Do not blame the driver. Lei ha detto 'al casino, per favore'; questa parola significa in italiano una casa, dove ci si diverte con delle belle ragazze. You said 'al casino, per favore'; this word means in Italian a house, where you can have fun with beautiful girls. Una casa, dove si gioca alla roulette, si chiama in italiano 'casinò'. A house, where you can play roulette is called in Italian 'casinò'

"Un accento sbagliato e le sue conseguenze", dice ridendo il signor Müller.

"A wrong accent and its consequences", says Mr. Müller laughing.

Vocabulary

above all sopra tutto
accept accettare
accident incidente m
accompany accompagnare
adapter adattatore m
address indirizzo
admission fee
ingresso m
admit
ammettere
advocate avvocato m
afternoon
pomeriggio m
age età f
air bed materassino m
conditioning aria
condizionata
air port aeroporto m
allergy allergia f
allow permettere
alone solo(a)
already già
also anche
always
sempre
ambulance ambulanza f
amount importo m
animal
animale m
answer rispondere
antique antichità f
apartment appartamento m
aperitif aperitivo m
apple mela f

arrive arrivare
art arte f
artificial
artist artista m f
arm braccio m
assurance
assicurazione f
ashtray
portacenere m
ask domandare
~ pregare
attention
attenzione f
August agosto m
autumn autunno
awake
svegliare
B
back schiena f
baggage bagaglio
bakery panetteria
balcony balcone
bank banca f
banknote
banconota f
basin lavandino
bath bagno m
bathrobe
accappatoio
battery batteria f
bay baia f
be essere
~ trovarsi
be called chiamarsi

be missing mancare
beach spiagga f
colazione f
bed letto m
beef manzo m
beer birra f
begin iniziare
beginning inizio m
behind dietro
belt cintura f
between fra, tra
bike
bicicletta f
bill
conto m
birthday compeanno m
biscuit biscotto m
blanket coperta f
bleed sanguinare
blood
sangue m
blue blu
boat barca f
body corpo m
bone osso m
book libro m
bookshop
libreria f
border frontiera f
born nato
borrow noleggiare
bottle bottiglia f
~ of gaz bombola del gas
box scatola f
boy ragazzo m

bread pane m
breakfast
bring portare
brochure
opuscolo m
broken rotto
broom scopa f
brother fratello m
bucket secchio m
bus autobus m
~ stop
fermata
dell'autobus
butcher's
macelleria f
butter burro m
button bottone m
buy comprare
~ acquisto m
by air mail per
posta aerea
C
cable car funivia f
cake torta f
~ shop pasticceria f
call chiamare
camera macchina
fotografica
camp campeggiare
can potere
cancel obliterare
candle candela f
car automobile f
car parc
parcheggio m

78

caravan roulotte f
carry portare
guardaroba m
case valigia f
cash desk cassa f
casino
casinò m
castle castello m
cathedral duomo m
cutlet scaloppina f
cemetery cimitero
centre centro m
century secolo m
certificate certificato m
chain chaîne catena f
chair sedia f
~ lift seggiovia f
change cambiare
charge tassa f
cheap conveniente
cheese formaggio m
checkroom
deposito bagagli
chicken pollo m
child
bambino(a)
chocolate cioccolato m
cinema
cinema m
clean pulire
~ pulito(a)
clock orologio m
close chiudere
cloth tessuto m
clothes vestiti m Pl

code prefisso m
cloakroom
coin moneta f
colleague collega
colour colore m
~ film pellicola a
colori
comb pett
come venire
come venire
complaint
reclamo
contain contenere
contract contratto
control controllare
cook cucinare
cooked cotto(a)
cost costare
cousin cugino(a)
cover coperto m
cream panna f
credit card carta di
credito
cross attraversare
cross-country
skiing
sci di fondo
~ski run pista di
fondo
cup tazza f
current corrente f
cut tagliare
D
day giorno m
dance ballare

danger pericolo m
dangerous
pericoloso(a)
 dark oscuro(a)
date data f
~ of birth
data di
 nascita
daughter figlia f
patente f
dentist dentista m f
December dicembre m
decision decisione f
deep profondo(a)
delay ritardo m
demonstrate dimostrare
department store
grandi magazzini m Pl
departure
partenza f
describe
 descrivere
diesel diesel m
different diverso(a)
difficulty difficoltá f
dinner
 cena f
direct diretto(a)
direction direzione f
dirty
sporco(a)
disappear sparire
discotheque discoteca f
discount
riduzione f

dog cane m
door porta f
double room
camera doppia
dress vestito m
drink bere
 drinking water
 acqua potabile
driving licence
patente f
drop goccia f
E
each ogni
ear orecchio m
Easter Pasqua f
eat mangiare
economy economia
egg uovo m
electric elettrico(a)
embassy
ambasciata f
emergency
 emergenza f
enough abbastanza
entrance entrata f
envelope busta f
escalator scala
 mobile
exchange cambio
excuse scusare
exhibition
esposizione f
exit uscita f
explain spiegare
express treno
 rapido

eye occhio m
F
face viso m
fair fiera f
fall cadere
family famiglia f
fashion moda f
 fat
grasso m
father padre m
February febbr
feel sentire
ferry traghetto m
film pellicola f
find trovare
finger dito m
finish finire
fire fuoco m
fish pescare
~ pesce m
fill out compilare
flat gomma a terra
fleamarket
 mercato delle pulci
flight volo m
floor piano m
flower fiore m
fog nebbia f
follow
 seguire
foot piede m
forbid vietare
forget dimenticare
fork forchetta f
form forma f

forward in avanti
fountain fontana f
France Francia f
French francese m
fresco affresco m
friend amico(a)
parucchiere m
fruit juice succo di
 frutta
full pieno(a)
funny comico(a)
fungus fungo m
G
gain guadagnare
gallery galleria f
garage officina f
garden giardino
gas gas m
get ricevere
~ procurare
~ on salire
~ out scendere
~ up alzarsi
gift regalo m
give dare
glass bicchiere m
glasses occhiali m
gold oro m
golf course campo
 da golf
go out uscire
gram grammo m
grandfather nonno
grandmother nonna
grill griglia f

group gruppo m
greet salutare
guide guida m f
guided tour visita f
guidata
H
hair
capello m
half metà f
~ mezzo(a)
~ board mezza
pensione
ham prosciutto m
hand mano f
~ bag borsetta f
hanky fazzoletto m
happy felice
harbour
porto m
harvest raccolta f
hat cappello m
have avere
have to dovere
health salute f
hear
sentire
heat
caldo m
heating
riscaldamento m
helicopter
elicottero m
help aiutare
help aiuto m
here qui, qua

history storia f
hold tenere
holiday
giorno festivo
holidays ferie f Pl
honey miele m
horse cavallo m
hospital ospedale
hotel albergo m
hour ora f
hours of business
orario d'apertura
hunger fame m
hurry fretta f
I
ice-cream gelato m
~ parlour gelateria
identity card carta
d'identità
kitchen cucina f
ill malato(a)
illness malattia f
immediately
subito
important
importante
inclusive
compreso(a)
infection infezione
inform informare
inhabitant abitante
inn trattoria f
inquire domandare
insect insetto m
instead of invece

interpreter interprete
invite invitare
iron stirare
island isola f
Italian italiano(a)
J
jam marmellata f
January gennaio m
jacket giacca f
jeweller gioielliere
journey viaggio m
juice succo m
July luglio m
June giugno m
K
key chiave f
kilometre
chilometro m
kind gentile
kiosk edicola f
knee ginocchio m
knife coltello m
knock bussare
know conoscere
~ ledge conoscenza
L
lady signora f
lake lago
lamb agnello m
lamp lampada f
last durare
laugh ridere
laxative lassativo
leather goods
pelleteria f

leave partire
leg gamba f
lemon limone m
lemonade limonata
less meno
let lasciare
letter lettera f
life vita f
~ belt salvagente m
~ guard bagnino m
lift ascensore m
light luce f
~ bulb lampadina f
lighter accendino
lip labbro m
~ stick rossetto m
liqueur liquore m
liquid liquido m
list lista f
litre litro m
live abitare
~ vivere
look sguardo m
look for cercare
lose perdere
loud rumoroso(a)
love amare
luck fortuna f
lunch pranzo m
luxurious lussuoso
M
magazine rivista f
man uomo m
March marzo m
market mercato m

marvellous
miracoloso
match fiammifero
material materiale
mattress materasso m
May maggio m
meal pasto m
mean significare
measure misurare
meat carne f
mechanic
meccanico m
medical insurance
company
assicurazione sanitaria
medicament
medicinale m
meet incontrare
menu menù m
message messaggio m
meter metro m
middle medio(a)
midnight
mezzanotte f
milk latte m
mineral water
acqua minerale
miniature golf minigolf m
minute minuto m
mirror specchio m
mist nebbia f
mistake errore m
mister signore m
mistress signora f
mix mescolare

mobile telefonino
moment momento
Monday lunedì m
money denaro m
month mese f
moon luna f
more più
morning mattina f
mother madre f
motor motore m
~ boat motoscafo
~ bike motocicletta
~ way autostrada f
mouth bocca f____
muscle muscolo m
museum museo m
music musica f
N
nail unghia f
~ scissors forbicina
name nome m
narrow stretto(a)
nationality
nazionalità f
neck nuca f
necessary
  necessario
need
avere bisogno di
never mai
newspaper giornale
New Year
capodanno m
next prossimo(a)
night notte f

non-alcoholic analcolico(a)
noon mezzogiorno
nose naso m
not non, no
nothing niente
now adesso
parapendio m
number numero m
nurse infermiera f
nut noce f
O
occupy occupare
offer offrire
office ufficio m
off season bassa stagione
oil olio m f
omelette frittata f
one si
one way street senso unico
only soltanto
open aprire
foperate funzionare
operation operazione f
opposite di fronte
optician ottico m
orange arancia f
order ordinare
other altro(a)
P
Paediatrician pediatra m
pain dolore m

paint pitturare
painter pittore m
painting pittura f
pair paio m
palace palazzo m
paper carta f
paraglider
parents genitori
park parcheggiare
park parco m
part parte f
party festa f
path sentiero
patience pazienza
patient paziente
pay pagare
~ in versare
pedestrian pedone
pepper pepe m
people gente f
per cent per cento
perfume profumo
perhaps forse
petrol benzina f
petrol-station stazione di servizio
pharmacy farmacia
phone telefonare
phone card scheda telefonica
piece pezzo m
pill pillola f
pillow guanciale
pity compatire
place luogo m

plan pianta f
plane aereo m
plant pianta
plaster cerotto m
plate piatto m
platform molo m
play giocare
~ gioco m
pleasant piacevole
please piacere
~ per favore
police polizia f
pocket tasca f
population
popolazione f
pork maiale m
porter portiere(a) m/f
portion porzione f
possible possibile
prefer preferire
present presente
press premere
price prezzo m
private privato
profession
professione f
programme programma m
pronounce pronunciare
protect conservare
pub trattoria f
pull tirare
punctual puntuale
pure puro(a)
purse
portamonete m

put mettere
Q
question domanda
quiet tranquillo(a)
R
rain piovere
~ coat
impermeabile
raw crudo(a)
razor rasoio m
reach raggiungere
read lire
ready pronto(a)
reception ricezione
recommend
raccomandare
red wine vino rosso
region regione f
religion religione f
rent dare in affitto
renting affitto
repair riparare
~ riparazione f
repeat ripetere
report denunciare
reserve prenotare
residence domicilio
restaurant
ristorante m
return tornare
~ ritorno m
rice riso m
ring suonare
river fiume m
roast arrosto

86

roll panino m
room sala f
round rotondo(a)
rubbish spazzatura f
~ bin pattumiera f
fmrucksack zaino m
S
safe cassaforte f
sail veleggiare
sailing boat barca a
 vela
salad insalata f
sale saldi mpl
~ vendita f
salmon salmone m
salt sale m
salutation saluto m
sand sabbia f
sanitary towel
sauce salsaf
sausage salsiccia f
say dire
scissors forbici fpl
sculptor scultore m
sculpture scultura f
sea mare m
m ~ food frutti di mare
season stagione f
seat posto m
see vedere
 ~ again rivedere
 sell vendere
send inviare
separate
separato (a)

serve servire
service
servizio m
shadow ombra f
shawl sciarpa
sheet lenzuolo m
ship nave f
shirt camicia f
shoe scarpa f
shop negozio m
~ window vetrina
shopping centre
ipermercato m
speed velocità f
 show mostrare
shower do ccia f
side dish contorno
sign firmare
signature firma f
single solo(a)
~ room
camera singola
sister sorella f
sit essere seduto
~ down sedersi
size taglia f
skating pattinaggio
skewer spiedino
sleep dormire
sleeper vagone
letto
slice fetta f
smoke fumare
smoker fumatore m
 soap sapone

87

sock calzino m
socket
presa di corrente
son figlio m
song canzone f
soon presto
sort sorta f
soup zuppa f
speak parlare
speaker
altoparlante m
spell sillabare
spice spezia f
spicy piccante
splendid splendido(a)
spoon cucchiaio m
spring primavera f
square piazza f
some alcuni(e)
spend spendere
stairs scala f
stamp francobollo m
starter
antipasto m
station stazione f
stay restare
~ soggiorno m
bistecca f
steal rubare
still ancora
stomach stomaco m
stop fermare
~ fermata f
straight ahead tutto diritto
stranger straniero(a)

street strada f
stupid stupido(a)
style stile m
sugar zucchero m
suit completo m
summer estate f
sun sole m
Sunday domenica f
suntan cream
crema solare
supermarket
supermercato m
surprise
sorprendere
surprise sorpresa f
swim nuotare
 T
table tavolo m
take prendere
take an interest
interessarsi
take away portare
take off decollo m
tax tassa f
tea tè m
team squadra f
television steak
televisione f
tent tenda f
terminal capolinea
terrace terrazza f
that questo(a)
thank ringraziare
theatre teatro m
theft furto m

there là, lì
there and back
andata e ritorno
thermometer
termometro m
think pensare
third terzo
thirst sete f
this questo
questa
though benché
Thursday giovedì m
ticket biglietto m
~ office biglietteria f
tide marea f
low ~ bassa marea
high ~ alta marea
time tempo m
time table orario m
tired stanco(a)
tobacco tabacco m
today oggi
together insieme
toilet paper
carta igienica
toll pedaggio m
tomato pomodoro m
tomorrow domani
tone tono m
too troppo
tooth dente f
toothpaste dentifricio m
touch toccare
tour
giro m

tourist office
ufficio del turismo
towel
asciugamano m
tower torre f
town città f
town hall
municipio m
traffic circolazione
 train treno m
transport trasporto
translate tradurre
travel viaggiare
treat curare
tree albero m
trolley carrello m
trousers pantaloni
try provare
Tuesday martedì m
tyre gomma f
U
ugly brutto(a)
umbrella ombrello
understand capire
unfortunately
sfortunatamente
unleaded senza
piombo
urgent urgente
use usare
V
valid valido(a)
vanilla vaniglia f
veal vitello m
 vegetable verdura

ventilator
ventilatore m
view vista f
ierivillage villaggio m
vinegar aceto m
visit visitare
visitors tax tassa di
 soggiorno
voltage tensione f
W
wait aspettare
waiter cameriere(a)
wake svegliare
wallet
portafoglio m
want volere
wash lavare
Wednesday
 mercoledì m
week settimana f
white wine vino
 bianco
whole tutto(a)
why perché
wife sposa f
wind vento m
wine vino m
winter inverno m
withdraw ritirare
 window finestra f
word parola f
woman donna f
work funzionare
working day
giorno feriale

Y
year anno m
yesterday
your
il tuo, la tua

<u>From the same author:</u>

French in 10 days -
Language course with a
new method

Publishing house:

Books on Demand
Norderstedt, Germany
2013

ISBN 9783732262595